# MIXED MARTIAL ARTS
## & COMBAT SPORTS

"The best fighter is not a Boxer, Karate or Judo man. The best fighter is someone who can adapt to any style, to be formless, to adopt an individual's own style and not follow the system of styles. The perfect style is no style. You take a little something from everything. You take the good things from every discipline, use what works and throw the rest away."

*Bruce Lee*

**CONTENT:**

# History of MMA

The history of MMA takes us back to the Olympics of Ancient Greece. The original sport was called Pankration, a Greek word meaning "all powers". This event was a gruelling mix of boxing and wrestling and the only rules were no eye gouging or biting.

All holds from wrestling and any blow from a boxer's arsenal were permitted. The Greek spectators worshipped the contestants, and they were treated as heroes, because they saw Pankration as the ultimate test of strength and technique.

Over the years, the different styles of fighting have all been practised within their own rules and forms of attack. This ranges from Boxing, a discipline that never goes to the ground, to Wrestling where there are no punches thrown, through to Tae Kwon Do, Judo, Aikido, Muay Thai, etc.

It was inevitable that one style would be brought together with another to see which was superior. Of course, when a grappler is matched against someone who is trained in the art of kicking, the fun begins. It wasn't until fighters started to take a bit from each of the styles - mixing Muay Thai, Boxing, Karate, Judo, Brazilian Jui Jitsu, Sambo, Kung Fu and Wrestling - that we now have the fastest growing sport in the world, Mixed Martial Arts.

It was also only a matter of time before this revival of interest in testing the skills of great fighters across many martial styles would evolve into formally staged sporting events, but few could imagine how that would come about and the spectacular rise in global popularity that would come with it. The vehicle that brought mixed martial arts to the world's attention was UFC.

UFC (Ultimate Fighting Championship) is celebrating 21 years as a powerful, engaging spectacle. It has evolved from humble beginnings in the early 90s to one of the most watched sports on the planet.

The origins of UFC are attributed to four characters who, by pooling their skills, were able to lay down the pillars of this wonderful art, and through sheer determination and against all odds, make it work.

Rorion Gracie, Art Davie, Campbell McClaren and Bob Meyrowitz are the original founders of UFC. When Art Davie heard about Rorion Gracie and Brazilian Jiu Jitsu he met up with him. Rorion was training family members and friends and about to start a new school in the USA.

Art Davie, a business entrepreneur known for producing advertisements in California, had read an article in *Playboy* magazine about a Brazilian Jiu Jitsu family called the Gracies. He had been toying with a new idea of presenting fighting to the public. He jumped on a plane and pitched his idea to Rorion Gracie. While he was considering the offer, Art produced some instructional videos of BJJ, which were an instant hit. This success got Rorion more interested in hearing about the original offer. Art then buddied up with Campbell McLaren, an executive producer, who instantly liked this weird new way of presenting fighting. The thought of one style matched against another reminded him of *Mortal Kombat*, a popular video game at the time. He could see great potential in promoting the no rules, anything goes tag. At that stage it was known as "War of the Worlds".

SHOULD IT
BE BANNED?

Originally promoted as "no-holds-barred, any rules", this turned out to be not entirely true. There were two rules: no eye gouging and no biting. However the publicity machine was in full swing pushing the two men enter and one comes out concept with great success.

Enter United States Senator John McCain, a popular politician, war hero and POW who, although a boxing fan, bitterly opposed the UFC from the very beginning. He branded it a "human cockfight", sensing danger on the horizon in what he called a blood sport.

McCain led a campaign to ban UFC, sending letters to the Governors of 50 states asking them to back the campaign. At first, UFC promoters saw it as great publicity, but it was not long before networks pulled the fast growing mega sport from their schedules.

The UFC had to move fast, and before long The Iowa Athletic Commission introduced new rules: 3-5 minute rounds with light shootfighting-style gloves, no hair pulling, no groin strikes or hits to the back of the head or neck and no head butting. Rather than gladiator warfare, it was promoted as the world's fastest growing sport.

Mixed martial arts was indeed taking over the world, with huge events being held not only in the USA but also Brazil, where it had started, and in Japan with what is now known as Pride Fighting being introduced in 1997. The first Pride Championships held at the Tokyo Dome attracted 50,000 fans as well as lots of media attention through Japanese television. Rickson Gracie and pro wrestler Nobuhik Takada were matched and Pride Fighting was born.

*Senator John McCain*

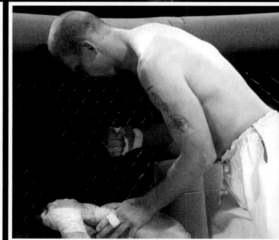

### ROYCE GRACIE

The son of Helio Gracie, and younger brother to Rorion, Relson and Rickson, Royce started competing in Brazilian Jiu Jitsu at the age of eight. While learning from his father and his brothers, he had received his Black Belt by the time he was eighteen. He went on to become the best grappler America had ever seen and dominated mixed martial arts throughout the 90s. Known for his great mental toughness and for staying calm when under incredible pressure, Royce emerged as a UFC legend.

### KEN SHAMROCK

Royce met his match when shootfighter and heavyweight champion Ken Shamrock entered the octagon and drew him in the UFC finals. Ken had great wrestling skills and was one of the few that had any experience against ground fighting, which at that time made him Royce's greatest rival. He soon earned the nickname as "the world's most dangerous man".

### GERARD GORDEAU

Another trophy winner in the early 1990's was Dutch Karate champion and Savate practitioner Gerard Gordeau.

He held the 1991 Savate championship and won the world tournament in Kyokushin Karate for eight consecutive years. He is best known for his famous 26 second win over Sumo giant Teila Tuli. The fight had to be stopped when Gordeau let go of a powerful kick that knocked out three of Tuli's teeth, two of them imbedding into Gordeau's foot. He continued to fight two more competitors with the teeth still in his foot, the doctors fearing that if they removed them there would be too much bleeding.

# UFC The Players

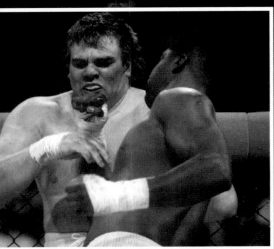

## ZANE FRAZIER

Kempo Karate King, Zane Frazier was classed as a heavyweight and stood at 1.98 metres, or 6'6" tall. He had won endless Karate tournaments before changing camps and entering the world of kickboxing, winning the WKF United States superheavy weight title in 1993. He met his match in UFC when he came up against Kevin Rosier in a messy brawl- like event where he was punched to the floor and kicked when he was on the ground. He was taken to hospital not long after, suffering from respiratory failure.

## ART JIMMERSON

Another great warrior was the gifted amateur boxing champion Art Jimmerson. Art had won the national Golden Gloves championship in 1983 and continued winning endless trophies after turning pro in 1985. He competed in the very first UFC challenge and lost to Royce Gracie after being taken down in the first round and then tapping out in the first two minutes.

## DAN SEVERN

Dan Severn, a UFC Hall of Famer and UFC Triple Crown champion, started his career as a Greco Roman wrestler having won the USA national championships twice. He was the guy to beat at college and was inducted into the Arizona State University Wrestling Hall of Fame. He entered the Octagon and impressed everyone with his freestyle wrestling skills, beating Anthony Macias. He too eventually went down to Royce Gracie. In 1995, he defeated Paul Varelan, Tank Abbott and Oleg Taktarok all on the same night to take the tournament title. Severn had a colourful history with MMA and went on to win through a brilliant submission hold on Aaron Garcia for his 100th career victory in 2011.

*Helio and Carlos Gracie*

# Brazilian Jiu Jitsu

Thought to originate in India around 2000 BC, early forms of martial arts were developed by monks for self-defence. It gradually moved into China and settled in Japan. Over centuries of evolution in Asia, techniques were split up and different styles emerged, such as Judo, Karate and Aikido. The Samurai adapted Jiu Jitsu as a way to defend in the unlikely case that they would be disarmed. In 1900, a man called Jigor Kana developed a style of fighting called Kodukan judo which blended throwing, grappling and striking techniques. Kana's top student, a successful Japanese businessman named Mitsuyo Maedo, decided to move to Brazil where a local politician named Gastro Gracie helped him to settle. Feeling like he should return the favour, Maeda started to teach Gastro's son Carlos Jujitsu, and found him to be an excellent student. He excelled and went on to teach his four brothers. In 1925, they opened a Jiu Jitsu academy in the heart of Brazil.

A few changes occurred over the years. Helio, at 16, was in poor health and with a light, small frame was unable to train. However he insisted on watching his brothers constantly improving and finding new ways to dominate. Helio was keen to overcome his disadvantage of a frail physique and started to modify the techniques that were working for others but not for him. It was Helio who introduced leverage and timing to Jiu Jitsu and went on to instruct, adapt and change so that it worked for him. Through constant experimentation he developed what we now know as Brazilian Jiu Jitsu.

Helio put out an open challenge to all the best Brazilian martial artists, and fought 18 times. He defeated all of them, including Wladek Zbyszko the world heavyweight wrestling champion.

He then went on to fight Masahiko Kimura, the best Jiu Jitsu fighter Japan had ever produced and who out-weighed Helio by 80 pounds. Helio was

*The blood choke*

defeated, but Kimura was so impressed with the techniques that Helio had used on him that he invited him back to Japan to teach.

BJJ differed in some ways to Judo and the original Jiu Jitsu, and the Gracie family found that some of the moves and techniques were fine for sport but they also needed to know that what they were practising was going to be applicable in the street. For example, when competing in a judo match, it could be won with a throw or a pin without a submission but in real life it just did not work. They soon fixed that.

# The ground is my friend

*Rear naked choke*

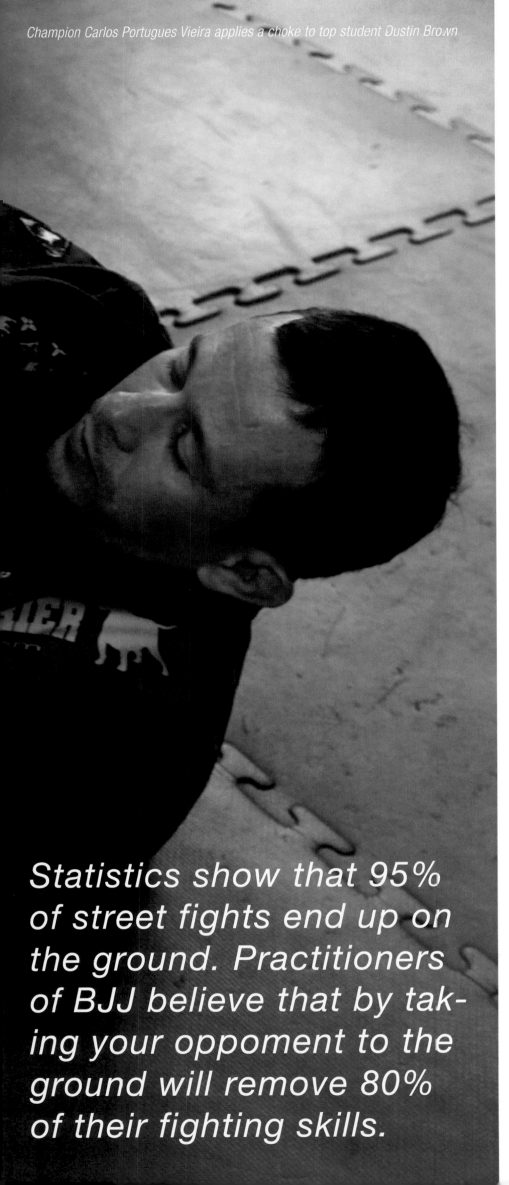

Champion Carlos Portugues Vieira applies a choke to top student Dustin Brown

*Statistics show that 95% of street fights end up on the ground. Practitioners of BJJ believe that by taking your oppoment to the ground will remove 80% of their fighting skills.*

# The blood choke is a form of strangulation that restricts the blood flow either through one or both of the carotid arteries that run down the side of the neck.

Brazilian Jiu Jitsu is divided into three categories: -

1. Self defence including strikes and unarmed techniques against weapons

2. Vale Tudo competition fighting, where anything goes and what has evolved into what we call MMA.

3. Sports grappling based on submissive holds with no striking.

Vale Tudo was introduced in the late 1950's, inviting all styles of martial arts to compete. It was soon known as "The Gracie Challenge". It wasn't long before it featured heavily on Brazilian television as *Ring Heroes* but it gained a reputation for violence and at times caused public disruption, so it soon went underground.

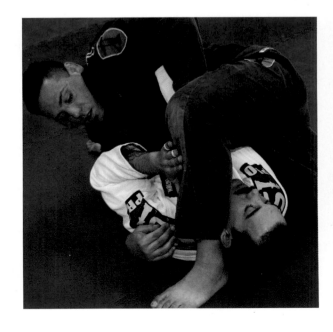

## CARLSON GRACIE

Weighing in at 70 kgs, Carlson Gracie Snr was one of the most renowned Brazilian fighters and had beaten or drawn with anyone who was up to the challenge by the time he was 23 years old. He went on to become a 9th degree red belt and was referred to as a Grandmaster.

Born in 1932 in Rio de Janeiro, Brazil, he was the son of the founder Carlos Gracie and started competing in BJJ at the age of five. Training all through his teenage years he turned professional at 18 and came up against Judo expert Sakai. Carlson. He weighed 67kgs, with Sakai coming in at 92kgs. It was called a draw as none managed to submit the other and after this bout Carlson put out the word that he would fight anyone in the country with all winnings going to drought victims of Brazil.

He went on to create one of the best academies in the country, producing endless champions and coaching the strongest team in Brazil's history: the Carlson Gracie Arrebentacao team.

Never holding back with his views and always a great character, his death in 2006 of heart failure surprised the Jiu Jitsu community.

## ROYCE GRACIE

Royce will be remembered as one of the best fighters of all time. He came to fame winning the first ever UFC championship despite his opponents consistently outweighing him. He went on to dominate MMA, winning 3 UFC titles and he still holds the record as the only man to defeat 4 opponents in a no holds barred match in one night. He continued to fight professionally in Japan, fighting Kazushi Sauraba in the longest MMA fight ever recorded, Judo Gold medallist Yoshida and Sumo champion Akebone, He defeated them all.

In 2003, Royce was inducted into the UFC Hall of Fame alongside old time rival Ken Shamrock. Today, Royce travels the world demonstrating and sharing brilliant techniques that his father Helio perfected. He currently oversees more than 55 US and international Jiu Jitsu networks.

# Philosophy & Training

The philosophy of BJJ is based on statistics that show that over 95% of street fights end up in the ground. Practitioners of BJJ believe that taking the opponent to the ground will remove 80% of the opponent's fighting skills, leaving those who have trained correctly a greater chance of finishing the job.

A BJJ training session is intense, with gruelling creative warm ups and drills that challenge even the most advanced students.

Being fit, supple, gaining core strength and developing body awareness are all factors that are essential when working closely with your training partner or adversary.

Similar in some ways to wrestling in its use of mount and guard, arm locks, leg, ankle, elbow and wristlocks are popular ways of submitting your opponent. Of course the trick is to avoid having others applying the same techniques to you. Staying relaxed, breathing and developing the vision to be able to see the next move coming are all tools that help you to endure.

*Victorian State Championships, Australia*

# Positions

Key positions used in BJJ are known as the mount, guard, side mount and north south scarf hold. There are also transitions such as standing up in base, side mount to front, Step over, push sweep (guard to mount), and double ankle grip sweep (guard to mount).

Some of the escapes are known as upward lift, guard escape (push) Guard escape (elbow drive), passing the guard (kneeling) and headlock escape.

With arm locks, there is Kimura from guard, mount side mount, shoulder lock from side mount, shoulder lock from scarf hold, arm bar from guard and mount.

# Take Downs

The ideal take down is when you are executing techniques that are high percentage, low risk and reasonably simple to execute. Dynamic explosiveness, flexibility, speed and strength are all part of the equation but timing is the main principle.

There are endless ways to take someone to the ground and one of the most popular is The Single Leg Takedown, which if executed correctly will certainly do the job. Placement of the head is important. Placing it between your opponents deltoid and neck area avoids the possibility of a guillotine choke. By placing the opponent's leg in-between yours and staying tight to his body, you engage your hips rather than utilising the arms, making the takedown seem effortless.

# The Sweep

The sweep can be used either from standing position or from the ground. From standing, sweeps are predominately throws that use the legs to attack opponent's legs.

One of the more popular standing sweeps is when someone grabs hold of you to grapple. Place your hand on the opponent's collar and the other under the opposite side elbow. Taking a step leading with the outside leg, place yourself next to your opponent and proceed to swing your inside leg behind him, returning the leg to the back of your opponent's as you push with your arms. At this stage one of your hands is clenching the front collar and the other has slid down from the elbow to the wrist as you make the throw.

# The Choke

There seem to be endless ways to submit a person in BJJ using the choke. The blood choke, the rear naked choke, triangle choke, GI choke guillotine, rear scissor and many more are used constantly both in real life situations or on the mat. When UFC first began, the public was astounded at how quickly, when using the Gracie's method of BJJ, an opponent would have to tap out. It sometimes left the spectators feeling that they hadn't got their money's worth from the event.

The blood choke is a form of strangulation that restricts the blood flow either through one or both of the carotid arteries running down the side of neck. A well-applied blood choke in just seconds can render a person unconscious without affecting the airways and using very little strength.

The air choke, sometimes called the "true" choke works differently than the blood choke and even though it is slower to cause unconsciousness, it does cause excruciating pain.

In BJJ, the chokes used not only apply pressure to the carotid arteries but also to the nerve bar receptors in the neck.

The person receiving can lose consciousness in about 3-5 seconds. The air choke however can take up to two minutes, depending on how long the person can hold their breath.

The future of BJJ is looking very positive, as schools directly connected to Brazil are opening in small towns and large cities worldwide. Kids are happily bowing to each other and shaking hands as they begin to grapple and learn from their devoted teachers. Women are getting more involved as they realize that this is an art that has proven time and time again that a light frame person can overcome a heavier adversary and have them submitted with very little effort in the most unusual and creative ways.

*Victorian State Championships, Australia*

# KARATE
## Master the Basics

*Sensei Brendan Fredericks demonstrates his no nonsense Koryo Shinjitsu-Ryu style response to top student Simon*

Karate arose from the indigenous fighting system of Okinawa known as Te. Around the 14th century, Chinese families settling on the island began to share their knowledge of Chinese arts and sciences, including Chinese Martial Arts. When weapons were banned for periods in 1429 and 1609, this furthered the development of unarmed combat techniques.

Karate developed from the synthesis of two fighting techniques: the first, a simple, practical and effective combat style arising from Te in Okinawa and the second, a more elaborate and philosophical style arising from the ancient culture of China. These dual origins of karate explain its violent efficiency coupled with its philosophical emphasis on discipline and nonviolence.

Sakukawa Kanga (1782 – 1838) was one of the first Okinawan practitioners to study in China and in 1806 began teaching a style called Tudi Sakukawa. One of his students, Itosu Anko, also known as "The Grandfather of Karate", developed new ways for less advanced students to perform their katas and this style became more mainstream.

The founder of Shotokan Karate, Gichin Funakoshi is known for popularizing Karate in Japan. He was a student of Itosu Anko and went on to get Karate accepted by the Japanese Budo organisation Dai Nippon Butoku Kai. Funakoshi trained in two styles, Shorin-Ryu and Shorei-Ryu. In 1936, he built a dojo in Tokyo and left behind his style called Shotokan.

# Full Contact

Masutatsu Oyama founded a new form of Karate in 1953, called Kyokushin. It is sometimes referred to as full contact Karate. Mas Oyama was in his prime at this stage of his life after spending many years in a remote area on Mt Kiyosumi training himself to overcome the challenges of solitude. He developed the ultimate challenge for himself with what is now known as the 100-men Kumite.

This was to be not only a test of physical endurance and strength but also mental stamina. Oyama would only set challenges to students of what he could overcome himself. He proceeded to organise the best of his black belts to attack him, one at a time for 2 minutes each and keep rotating until the total was 100 bouts. He was not happy to leave it at that; he did it for 3 days in a row totalling 300 bouts. In fact, he wanted to continue and do a fourth day but could not proceed due to lack of willing students. Some of them had been knocked out with a single punch and were still feeling the effects.

He earned a name for himself over the years for his battles with bulls. All together he would fight 52

bulls, killing 3 instantly and removing the horns of 49 with knife-hand strikes.

The first school outside Japan opened in 1957, by Mas Oyama's senior student Shihan Bobby Lowe, in Hawaii.

By 1964, the name of Kyokushin "The Ultimate truth" had evolved and become famous worldwide. To this day it is one of the largest martial arts organisations in the world.

## "If someone asked me what a human being ought to devote the maximum of his life to, I would say: Training. Train more than you sleep"

*Mas Oyama*

# Philosophy

The Japan Karate Association describes true Karate as a way of life that trains a practitioner to be peaceful and only when conflict is unavoidable does he or she resort to action. This requires the student to be not only focused and in control, but also fast and strong.

True karate is based on Bushido, where the whole person, body, mind and spirit are developed simultaneously. This harmonious ability to blend is extremely powerful, the result being confidence, humility and peace only coming to those who have perfect unity of mind and body.

*Goju practitioners performing a Kata*

# Karate Techniques

The basic technique is known as Kihon, followed by the Kata, or form, and then Kumite (sparring). They basically work as one, starting with Kihon. Once this is mastered, the student moves on to Kata, a series of movements that are repeated over and over, helping the body to memorise and move automatically without effort. The idea of Kumite is to react to situations naturally and freely whilst applying techniques without having to think and plan.

The fundamental techniques of karate are striking, kicking, punching and blocking. Many think that these simple moves can be easily executed but it can be a lifetime of work to master them.

When delivering a strike, all parts of the body must be in tune with each other to provide the stability necessary to sustain the shock of the delivery. Balance is paramount, hence the wide stance giving a lowering of the centre of gravity.

Below: Chief instructor 7th dan of Goju Ryu Kakann Kan Karate James Sumurac conducting a class

Training at the Wu Lin Retreat

However this changes depending on circumstances, and even though stability is important, the practitioner must be able to transfer weight and kick, sometimes balancing on one leg. Changing from one leg to another is one way of not staying for too long on one leg, with the constant change of the centre of gravity helping to prevent the opponent from capitalising.

The correct relationship between the feet and the floor is essential as Karate starts from the ground. Making use of not only the legs but also the ankles, knees and hips all ensure that a kick is powerful and the stance is stable.

Students realize quickly how important timing is in applying techniques; too early or too late both have poor outcomes. This is why sparring and working with a partner is essential, so that you can not only experiment with the power of your delivery, but whilst under pressure you can practise your timing and work on how to adjust according to the speed of the attack.

## CONDITIONING

Karate has earned a reputation for its rigor in training and preparation with breaking boards, bricks, roof tiles, concrete slabs and even coconuts. Strikes with the edge of the hand, fist, elbow and even head are all used to:

1) Help measure the power of your technique.

2) To get used to the impact of hitting solid objects with maximum force.

3) To develop accuracy at speed.

## SHUTO UCHI

Over the years, many have become familiar with the famous Karate chop or Shuto Uchi (knifehand strike) seen in the movies. This is just one of the many strikes in the immense repertoire of techniques. Knifehand is one of the most effective weapons of old Okinawa karate, especially when aimed at the throat. It can also be used to attack the opponent's face and limbs and can be used when being attacked by parrying the opponent's attack with your other hand and counterattacking simultaneously.

Closed fist punches, palm strikes, eye gouges, knee and elbow strikes, slaps and grabs are just some of the ways karate responds to an opponent's attack. Most people are unaware that karate is not just palm strikes and open

handed chops but does everything from elbow locks to head manipulation take downs, shoulder throws and scissor takedowns.

## UNSHU GERI

The scissor takedown or Unshu Geri can only work effectively if you are very agile, so you can kick well. Falling suddenly to avoid the opponents attack, you must place yourself in the correct position so that you can kick the attacker's groin whilst the other leg hooks the ankle of your opponent. The leg that you have used to kick then returns to the back of the knee creating the scissor take down. Often used when you are already on the ground.

## FUMI KIRI

When attacked with a wild haymaker a basic throw technique or Fumi Kiri can be very effective. There are a few different ways to respond to this but first you must time it so that you are catching the attack before it gathers full momentum.

Grabbing the inside elbow and the other hand placed either on the front of the attacker's shoulder, or use that hand to push the chin upwards. You must sweep the opponent's leg, taking him to the ground whilst maintaining the grip on his arm to control him.

## KENTEKI GERI

Sometimes the best defence is offence. When attacked with a kick, don't try and block it. This technique is called Kenteki Geri. Step aside and parry the attack, delivering a kick to the groin. Accuracy is paramount here, you don't have to kick hard to do damage. If you go for power it may slow you down.

## TOMOE NAGE

Another familiar technique that is often used in movies is known as Tomoe Nage or great wheel.

Originally used in Jiu Jitsu and sometimes called the sacrifice throw, the idea is to fall backwards onto your back, extending your leg into the opponents mid section and throw him over your head.

This technique is particularly effective when grabbed by the lapels or the chest.

# Karate Techniques

## PUNCHING

The first thing a student must learn about punching is to maintain good balance. If you don't have correct balance you cannot deliver an effective powerful punch. Speed is essential but it must be combined with mass in order to deliver power.

A strong stable stance is essential but the practitioner must also develop his ability to throw a punch whilst moving. Probably the greatest asset a student has after years of training is his will and self-belief. Karate students work extremely hard on developing the correct mindset through focus, meditation and self-reflection.

## KICKING

The size and the strength of the legs make kicking extremely powerful when executed correctly. Often, to maximise the effect, a sudden change in speed is added at the end of the technique and is aimed at the smallest striking area, concentrating the impact on a single point.

With the thrust kick your leg comes to an immediate stop as it impacts, locking the kicking knee into position. A snap kick makes use of a striking action that returns as soon as contact is made.

One of the reasons why kicks can be so effective is they are driven by the powerful muscles in the legs and the distance travelled during the kicking action builds a large amount of momentum. The snap kick then uses a sharp recoil to reverse the direction of the strike at the moment of impact. The reason why the impact is not reabsorbed in the body is the short time the foot makes contact with the target prevents any unbalancing. The ball and the edge of the foot, the heel and the instep are all used as weapons. They can be delivered with one foot on the ground or both in the air coming from any direction. The "pull back" creates power in the same way a whip does.

The thrust kick on impact locks the body and kicking leg into position to redirect the counter shock of the blow to the floor.

Most thrust kicks are kept low because of balance but some experienced practitioners who have good control over their body and understand direction of force find this kick extremely effective.

The locked off leg positions that we see in practise are designed to help execute a technique against an imaginary opponent whilst performing a Kata. The stances are held longer and this is not what is used in a real life situation. With sparring a free flowing series of movements are applied, not rigid posturing.

**The size and the strength of the legs make kicking extremely powerful when executed correctly.**

*Sebastien Aucher training at Don Millar's Supa Fight Gym*

# The Science of Eight Limbs

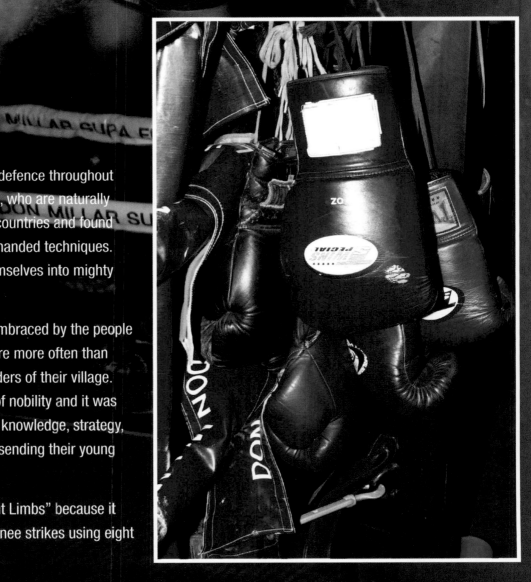

Muay Thai has been used as a form of self-defence throughout Thailand's colourful history. The Thai people, who are naturally gentle, were surrounded by not so friendly countries and found themselves developing weapons and open handed techniques. Throughout the ages, they transformed themselves into mighty warriors.

When Buddhism spread from India it was embraced by the people of Thailand. A community of monks that were more often than not retired soldiers were seen to be the leaders of their village. These men were the wise elders and men of nobility and it was their knowledge of the martial arts, military knowledge, strategy, sociology and psychology that had parents sending their young boys to them to learn the art of Muay Thai.

Muay Thai is known as the "Science of Eight Limbs" because it makes use of punches, kicks, elbows and knee strikes using eight points of contact.

# History

It wasn't until about 1700 AD that King Prachao Sua introduced Muay Thai as a sport away from the battlefield. He was a great competitor and would visit villages and set up competitions. He fought incognito and usually beat the local champions. It was from this that the great art of Muay Thai started as a sport and has evolved into the tapestry of the Thai culture.

Nearly all the young men of Thailand grow up learning Muay Thai Boxing as it is the nation's number one sport. The military also choose it, as it is so effective for close combat, with training camps set up all over the country.

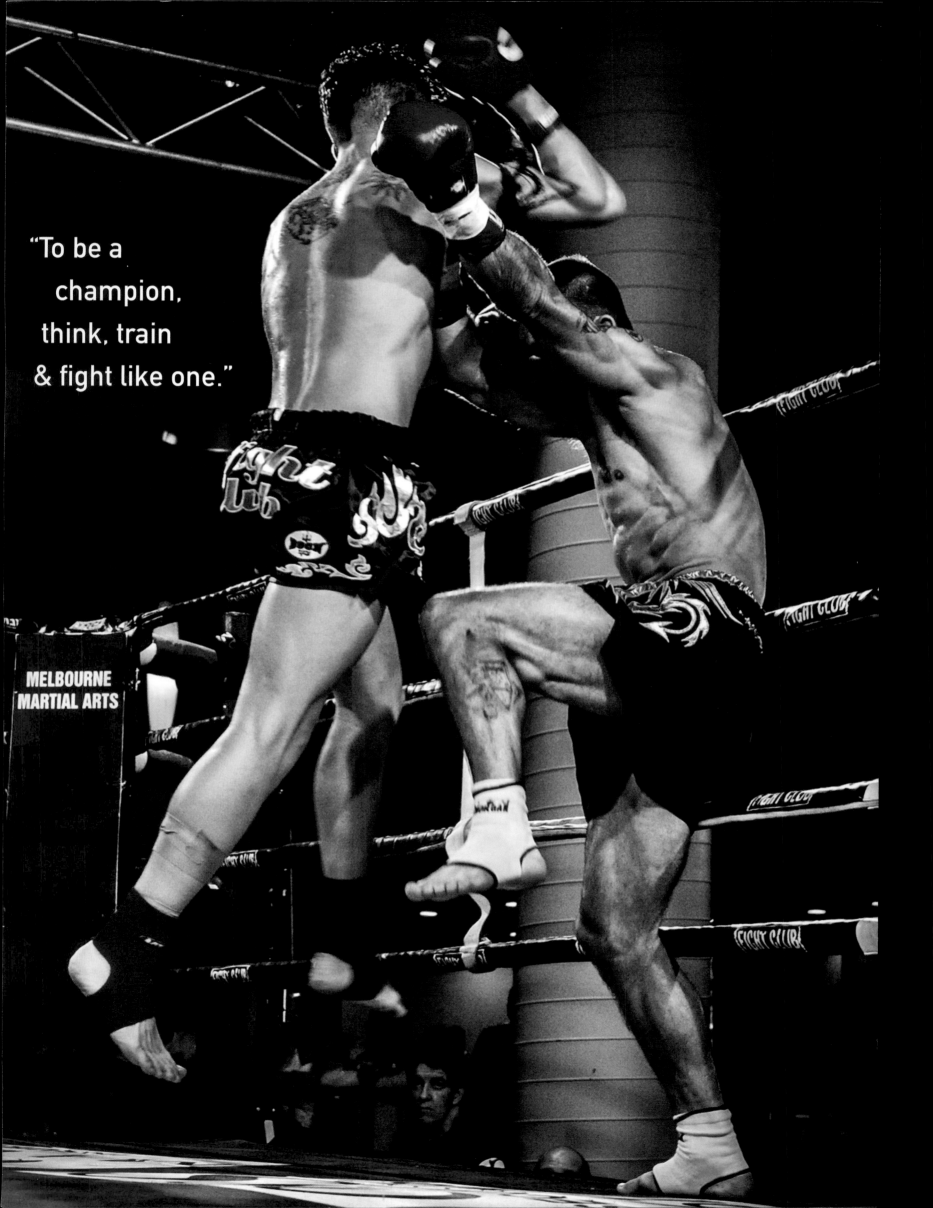

"To be a
champion,
think, train
& fight like one."

In the 1930s, Queensberry Rules and boxing gloves replaced the rope bindings on the boxer's hands, weight divisions were introduced, rules and regulations were fine-tuned and Muay Thai was officially codified and recognised as a safe ring sport.

A typical Thai boxing match lasts for 5 rounds of 3 minutes each, with 2 minute rests between rounds. In 1955 the first televised Muay Thai fight was broadcast from Kajadamnern stadium and soon attracted different styles of martial artists to challenge what was now the national sport of Thailand. The Thai fighters ruled, as competitors could not deal with the power of the Muay Thai kicks. It is seen to be superior to international boxing as not only fists but also elbows, knees and feet are used. At one stage the head was included in a boxers arsenal but this has been changed.

# Posture

The position of the head is slightly inclined with the chin tucked inside the shoulder line and the eyes focused on either the chest or the mid-section, unlike other martial arts where in most cases the eyes are set on the shoulders to read the body and general movements. The shoulders are slightly raised for protection and the elbows are placed quite close to the body, but not too high so you can protect the trunk.

The stance is not hunched or stooped but quite upright where the body is turned to the side to offer less target with all potential vulnerable target points covered. The hands are loosely clenched and raised to protect the face. Legs are slightly bent to allow immediate response to opponent's kicks.

The less skilful foot is positioned in the front with the toes pointed towards the opponent whilst the most skilful foot is placed with the toes pointed at a 45-degree angle. The heels are slightly lifted and balance is maintained through a natural shifting of the weight between the balls of the feet. The hands are positioned with the less skilful hand raised to the eyebrow level, with the arm extended a little facing the same direction as the foot, whilst the more skilful hand is raised to the level of the cheek with the palm towards the cheek.

## ELBOWS

Muay Thai boxers are encouraged to use elbows as it suits the close range boxing style. When the opponent steps forward and throws a committed punch with his right hand, the idea is not to retreat but move inside, raising your left hand to your ear to protect yourself. This position is perfect to apply an elbow strike to your opponent's ear or lower jaw. Correct timing is essential and you have to be aware of the opponent's other hand as you enter.

Another response to the same attack is to protect yourself with your left hand from an incoming right hand punch and step forward so you are close enough to apply an uppercut to the chin using the elbow. If you make the strike visible with your fists, your opponent lifts his head in response and you follow through with the elbow.

Another way to make use of the elbows is when you are attacked with a kick to the mid section with the opponent's right leg. Move inside the leg and drive down in a stabbing motion with both elbows. One elbow strike to the upper thigh muscle and the other to the shin.

Muay Thai fighters are extremely athletic and advanced practitioners might use some unusual responses to a kick to the mid-section.

The opponent attacks with a knee strike to the abdomen. The defendant jumps up using the advancing leg as a step, placing his foot on the attacker's thigh and placing his other foot on the attacker's shoulder, striking to the top of the head with an elbow blow.

This technique is still used in Thailand but has been banned in other countries.

## KNEES

### Straight Knee Kick

This technique illustrates one way of using the knee to counter an attack to the throat. The attacker advances with a left foot forward and attempts to grab the throat using the left hand. The defender brings both hands up to parry and leans back slightly, planting his knee in the attacker's abdomen. It is important to thrust your hips forward and you should be on the ball of your foot on

contact. The leg that is kicking should have the toes pointed to the ground as the knee impacts.

### Diagonal Knee Kick

The diagonal knee kick is similar to the straight knee kick and in most cases is executed by grabbing the opponent's neck with both hands. The knee is raised to attack from a diagonal direction and can be delivered to the thigh, rib and the side of the body.

A great place to kick your opponent with your knee is in the

side of the ribs above the hips. This can often be exposed after a punch has been thrown and still has a lot of tension in that area making it very vulnerable.

### Horizontal Knee Kick

With this technique it is best when you grab the opponent's neck with one hand, keeping the other hand ready. The knee is swung horizontally, keeping it horizontal to the ground. The hip is engaged, twisting in the same direction as the knee, ensuring a powerful strike.

### Knee Slap

This is probably the most popular technique used and is simply both hands grabbing the opponent behind the neck and using the inner part of the knee joint whilst raising the leg and slapping it into the target.

### Step up Knee kick

This knee kick uses your lead leg to step onto the attacker's thigh when he advances and raising your body up to thrust the knee of the other leg into your target, usually the face or chin. It is not used a lot as it is difficult to maintain your balance and requires a high degree of athleticism.

Muay Thai fighters do extensive conditioning from a very early age whilst their bones are forming, helping to strengthen their forearms and shins by building up the callus so that they become effective blocking utensils. Muay Thai fight techniques are practised consistently over and over again. By constantly drilling the techniques, the nervous system remembers how you throw and execute a delivery, each time you defend yourself with a kick or a punch, your body remembers, how it felt, how you did it and how long it took. The more you do, the better it gets!

In western fighting, the clinch is disallowed in the ring and the referee is quick to separate the competitors. Not so in Muay Thai. Holding the back of the neck or body is often used whilst the practitioner kicks with the knee. Low and mid kicks are normally blocked with a raised shin and mid to high are blocked with the forearm as well as the knee. The low kicks when executed use a rotational movement of the whole body to hit the opponent's outer thigh or the side of the knee. Old style training for the legs was to kick banana trees. The porous nature of the plant was ideal for practising leg kicks and knee strikes as it was soft enough not to damage the fighter's legs but hard enough to strike with force many times before collapsing. Fighters were known to roll small logs along the shins or hit them with sand bags building calluses and toughening the skin. Hanging coconuts in a row and striking, using fists, elbows and knees whilst they were moving were used to improve accuracy. Walking through strong currents in streams would also help build leg strength, along with digging a pit in the ground and jumping in and out help to provide the fighters the explosive power in their legs to execute kicks.

# PRE-FIGHT RITUAL

In Thai culture the head is seen to be the most important part of the body and when the fighter enters the ring he will always go over the rope never under. This is a symbolic gesture, as the head should never go beneath anything.

Each fighter wears a Mongkon; a traditional headband made from cotton yarn and is used to represent the camp or gym that the fighter represents. Fighters are never to touch the Mongkon. It can only be placed or removed by their Kru or trainer.

Muay Thai fighting is deeply connected to tradition and its cultural roots date back several centuries. One of the rituals performed before each fight is what is known as The Wai Kru/ Ram Muay, which is a ritualistic and traditional dance designed to honour the fighter's instructors, the sport itself and the country. These dances also allow the fighter to loosen up, relax and release tension and prepare the mind for combat.

# BOXING
## The Art of Fist Fighting

'Queensberry Rules'
Sullivan and Kilrain 1899

ENICE

Photo shows a crowd gathered for a boxing match at night, part of the 1907 exhibition
tour by Sullivan and Kilrain, who performed at the White City in July. (Source: Chicago Daily
Tribune, display ad, July 28, 1907)

The origins of boxing, also known as pugilism, go back to both ancient Greece and Rome. Not a lot is known about the way it was conducted back then. Much later, in 1681, The Duke of Albermarle in Britain organised the first official "boxing match". Originally bare knuckles were used but too many casualties occurred and in 1743 the first set of rules were published. They lasted until 1865 when John Sholto Douglass the Ninth Marquess of Queensberry established new rules of boxing, giving us what is now known as "The Queensberry Rules".

## The Rules

The popularity of boxing flourished and for the first time was included in 1904 at the St. Louis Olympic Games. Using the Queensberry rules, a roped off area of 24 feet, known as a ring, was established. The rounds were to be 3 minutes, with a 1-minute break between rounds, and no wrestling or hugging.

A fair sized set of gloves had to be worn and the only other person allowed in the ring was the referee.

The winner was determined when either man fell through weakness and was unable to get up unassisted within a ten second count, with the other boxer declared the winner.

In 1927, The National Boxing Association became the sport's first sanctioning body and would go on to arrange matches and rank fighters. Today there are three recognized sanctioning bodies that control the boxing world: the World Boxing Council, the International Boxing Federation and the World Boxing Association.

In the sport today, two competitors exchange blows with gloves and try to avoid being hit by the other. There are separate weight divisions and whilst amateur fights are made up of 3 rounds, in professional boxing the recognized length is 12 rounds. The rules may vary in different countries, sometimes making it quite controversial. These days the winner is determined by either a decision by the judges, the referee or both.

*Jack johnson*

*Sugar Ray Robinson*

## JACK JOHNSON

In 1908 Jack Johnson became the first black man to become heavyweight champion of the world. The media and the publicists had a field day setting up rivalry amongst blacks and whites.

America began to scour the country searching for a "great white hope". They found undefeated heavyweight champion James J. Jeffries, but not all went to plan and Jack Johnson retained his title.

Boxing was growing at a great rate, as Johnson, who was loud and flamboyant, became a huge celebrity and helped to gain boxing an even larger following.

## SUGAR RAY ROBINSON

The next big name to emerge in the 40s was Sugar Ray Robinson who, after turning pro in 1940, went on to astound the boxing world by winning his first 40 fights. Over 25 years Robinson racked up 175 wins, with 110 knockouts, and in 1946 won his bout with Tommy Bell, taking the crown with a unanimous 15 round decision. Six years later, at what was called "The St Valentine's Day Massacre", he defeated

Jake La Motta and became middleweight champion of the world. He continued to amaze the world with a 91 match unbeaten streak from 1943 to 1951, during which he also captured the welterweight title. Known for his flashiness, expensive suits, personal barbers and pink Cadillacs, Robinson grew accustomed to the good life and would become the first boxer with true celebrity status.

## ROCKY MARCIANO

While Robinson dominated the lower weight classes, a big hitter from Massachusetts called Rocky Marciano set the stage for arguably the greatest heavyweight boxer of all time.

Trainer Charley Goldman taught Marciano his trademark moves, and in 1951, with 37 wins and 32 knockouts under his belt, he faced his childhood hero heavyweight champ Joe Louis. Louis, past his prime by now, wasn't any match for Marciano and was beaten in the 8th round. Marciano went to Louis's dressing room after the fight and was seen crying as he was so upset for his boyhood idol.

In 1952, he defeated Jersey Joe Walcott in the 13th round by knocking

Rocky Marciano

Muhammed Ali

Mike Tyson

him unconscious, earning himself the championship belt.

## MUHAMMED ALI

Cassius Clay wanted nothing else but to be the heavyweight champion of the world. Joe Martin, his first trainer, said it was hard work and quick thinking that set him apart from the rest. Even before he was 18 years old he had won 6 Kentucky and 2 National Golden Gloves championships as well as 2 National AAU titles. After turning 18 he won the Olympic Gold Medal in 1960 in Rome.

Known for his powerful legs and dancing style, Cassius created what was known as "the Ali shuffle" and would concentrate on aiming for the head rather than body shots. He went on to defeat the awesome Sonny Liston in Miami and became heavyweight champion of the world. Soon after, he converted to Islam and changed his name to Muhammed Ali.

In 1971 he took on Joe Frazier at Madison Square Garden in a bout viewed in 35 counties across the world. It went the full 15 rounds and Ali appeared slower than before, losing the heavyweight title.

The "Rumble in the Jungle" was the most publicised fight of the century and was held in 1974 in Zaire, Africa. George Foreman was the overwhelming favourite to win but Ali had different ideas, and in the eighth round took out Foreman and made famous his rope-a-dope technique. Muhammad Ali left his mark on history and is seen by many to be the greatest boxer that ever lived.

## MIKE TYSON

A truly scary character, Tyson ruled the ring as undisputed world heavyweight champ from 1987-1990. Not since Muhammad Ali had retired had there been anyone that captured the media's attention for his power and technique in the ring and his controversial private life that dominated the sport headlines.

At only 20 years old he was the youngest man in history to claim the heavyweight championship title. He won his first 19 professional fights by knockout and held the championship titles in WBA, WBC and IBF titles. He left his mark on the boxing world, retiring in 2006 and was considered one of the best heavyweight boxers.

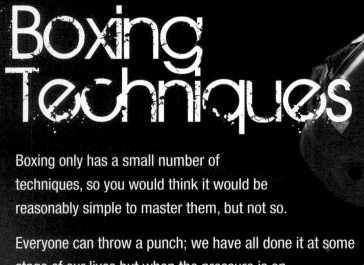

# Boxing Techniques

Boxing only has a small number of techniques, so you would think it would be reasonably simple to master them, but not so.

Everyone can throw a punch; we have all done it at some stage of our lives but when the pressure is on and the adrenalin kicks in, can your punch be accurate, fast, powerful and effective?

We would like to think so, but it takes years and years to gain the experience to use the right punch at the right time from the right distance. What makes boxing so fantastic is the great use of position, distance and cover. Once you have a handle on these basics the fun begins, as you start to mix and blend your combinations of jabs, crosses, hooks and uppercuts. Of course you can only do so much on the bag, as it doesn't hit back.

## THE JAB

The Jab was designed to keep your opponent at a distance and to feel out your range. Throwing the punch in a direct line just under your chin, make sure you rotate the fist, relaxing throughout the movement until the end when it is fully clenched. Then snap back to guard position.

## THE RIGHT CROSS

The Right Cross (Straight Right) is thrown with the right hand and is often used as a follow up to the jab.

Standing in a normal fighters stance throw the right hand from the chin guard position, turning your torso into the punch whilst pivoting on the right foot. You will gain more power if you accelerate your speed as your right heel pivots outward. Relaxing the hand after impact and returning to guard position.

## THE UPPERCUT

The Uppercut can also be very effective and in most cases takes the opponent by surprise. From guard position place your elbow so it rests on your left hip and launch upwards with the left side of the body rotating your left fist upwards.

Being a sport, fitness is a big part of the boxing preparation as there are weight divisions and time restraints. So stamina is essential for when the master plan to knock out your opponent in the first round doesn't go quite right and you find yourself gasping for air, getting a stitch and slowly losing power with every attempt to land the big one.

## THE LEFT HOOK

The left hook is a very effective punch often resulting in knockdown and works best when working close to your opponent.

Transfer your weight to the left side and from the guard position your elbow is raised and should be parallel with the floor, at this stage your arm should be imitating the shape of a hook. On execution the fist rotates and the punch is thrown pivoting on the left foot.

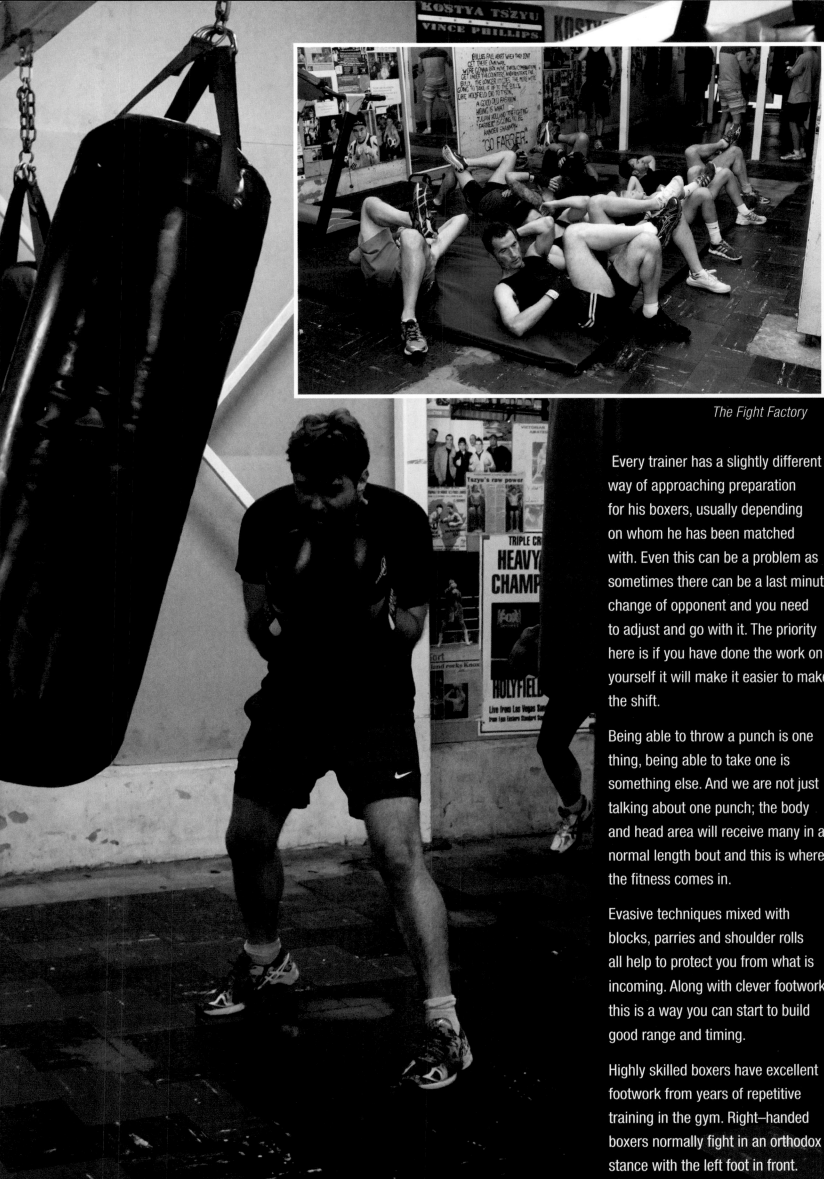

*The Fight Factory*

Every trainer has a slightly different way of approaching preparation for his boxers, usually depending on whom he has been matched with. Even this can be a problem as sometimes there can be a last minute change of opponent and you need to adjust and go with it. The priority here is if you have done the work on yourself it will make it easier to make the shift.

Being able to throw a punch is one thing, being able to take one is something else. And we are not just talking about one punch; the body and head area will receive many in a normal length bout and this is where the fitness comes in.

Evasive techniques mixed with blocks, parries and shoulder rolls all help to protect you from what is incoming. Along with clever footwork, this is a way you can start to build good range and timing.

Highly skilled boxers have excellent footwork from years of repetitive training in the gym. Right–handed boxers normally fight in an orthodox stance with the left foot in front.

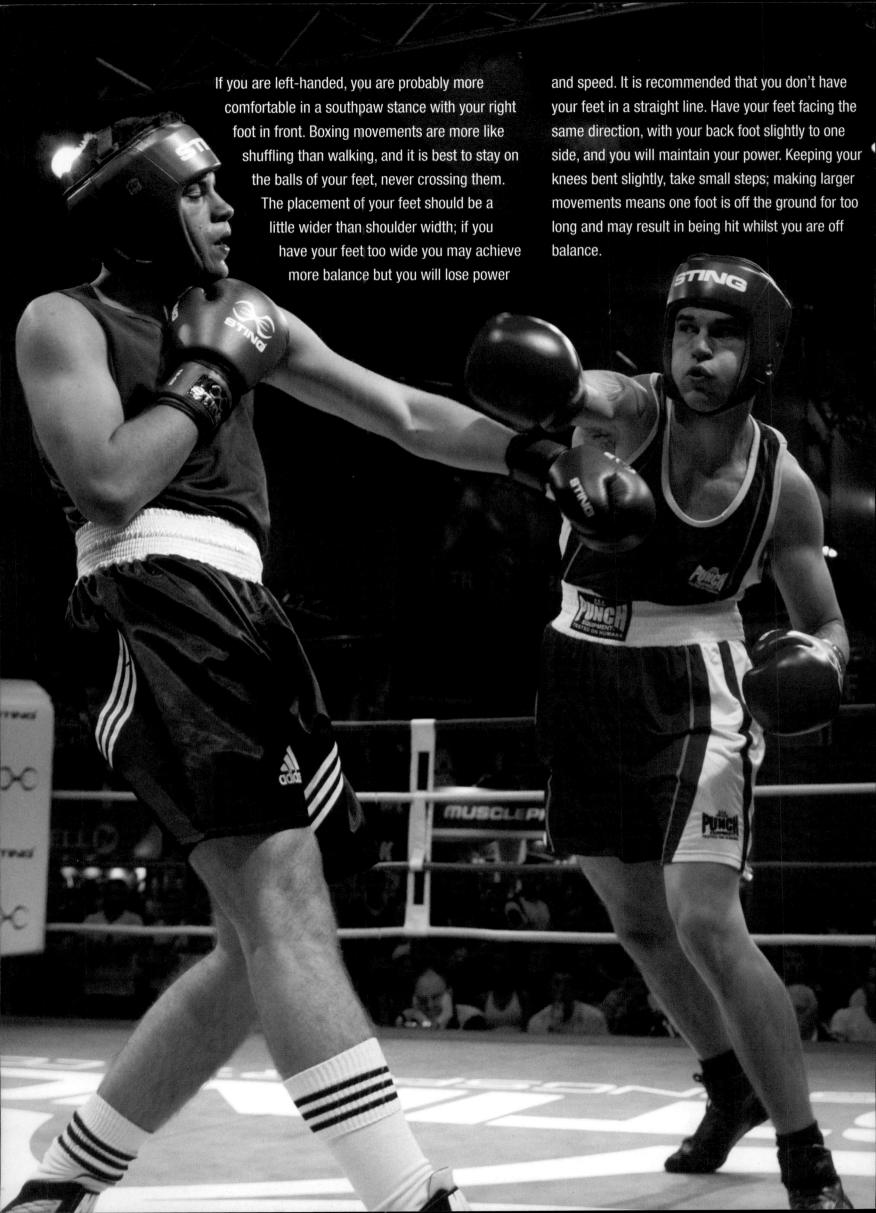

If you are left-handed, you are probably more comfortable in a southpaw stance with your right foot in front. Boxing movements are more like shuffling than walking, and it is best to stay on the balls of your feet, never crossing them. The placement of your feet should be a little wider than shoulder width; if you have your feet too wide you may achieve more balance but you will lose power and speed. It is recommended that you don't have your feet in a straight line. Have your feet facing the same direction, with your back foot slightly to one side, and you will maintain your power. Keeping your knees bent slightly, take small steps; making larger movements means one foot is off the ground for too long and may result in being hit whilst you are off balance.

"Boxing is the ultimate challenge. There's nothing that can compare to testing yourself the way you do every time you step in the ring"

*Sugar Ray Leonard*

# SAMBO

## Russia's Grappling Art

*Melbourne Open Sambo Grappling Competition, Australia*

The origins of Sambo are from Russia. It is similar in many ways to Judo and Jujitsu with some Russian wrestling techniques added to make a very effective martial art used by the elite Soviet forces and KGB agents for hand-to-hand self defense. Sambo meaning "self-defense without weapons " also has roots in folk styles of wrestling such as Armenian Kokh, Georgian Chidaoba, Mongolian Khapagay and many others. The man who introduced Sambo to Russia was Vasili Oschephov, who was one of the first Judo practitioners. The government promoted the sport throughout USSR and Europe in the same way Judo had been, and though soldiers were using it initially, it was sanctioned and officially made a sport. Sambo is one of the only four forms of wrestling practiced in international competitions, the others are Freestyle wrestling, Greco Roman Wrestling and Judo.

# The Sambo Goal:

## To stop an armed or unarmed attacker in the least time possible

*Sambo Master and 5th Dan Judo Instructor Coach Natalia Kuligina takes her students through their paces*

# Sambo History

Another of the pioneers was Victor Spiridinov who had a background in various arts and after receiving a serious injury from a bayonet wound in the First World War found using movement rather than strength was more effective. The style he worked towards was softer, utilizing an opponent's strength by deflecting their aggression in a direction they had not planned on going. Spiridinov and Oschepov did not agree on everything, leading to every technique being broken down and tested to make sure that it was suitable to achieve the Sambo goal: to stop an armed or unarmed attacker in the least time possible. Once the techniques were perfected they were integrated into the Sambo system and used for personal self-defense, police work, military, commando and bodyguard work.

During the 1920's and 1930's, the Russian Government conducted an investigation into the most effective fighting styles. They researched and dissected every martial art from every nation in an effort to develop the best hand-to-hand system. They decided that wrestling was the most effective defensive approach and combined Greco-Roman or Freestyle wrestling with Boxing, French Savate, Jiu Jitsu, Mongolian wrestling and bayonet fighting to produce one of the most comprehensive forms of fighting, renaming it Russian Sambo.

Even though the Russian authorities sought to create a completely new style with Sambo, many of its combat elements still had their origins in the Russian predecessor, Systema, the combat system developed by the elite army corps, the Spetsnaz.

In 1981 the International Olympic Committee recognized Sambo as an Olympic sport.

*Ccmpetitors at the Melbourne Open Sambo Grappling Competition, Australia*

## THE SAMBO STYLE

There are three main characteristics of Sambo.

1. Takedowns that combine a mixture of judo and wrestling techniques.
2. Ground skills
3. Leg locks

Sport Sambo allows every different type of leg lock and Sambo has developed a reputation for specializing in this. Much like Judo, takedowns and defense in being taken down are the main features of Sport Sambo.

**Combat Sambo** originated in the military and includes striking, kicking and grappling, using weapons and weapons disarming.

**Self Defense Sambo** includes ways of defending against weapons and using the attacker's aggression against them, much like Aikido and Jiujitsu.

**Freestyle Sambo** was created so non-Sambo participants could enter Sambo events (Judo and Jiu-jitsu practitioners) with some rule changes, including allowing the use of chokes and other submission moves that are not used in Sports Sambo.

Sambo's effectiveness lies in the ability of the practitioner to make use of natural body movements and rather than relying on practice of repetitive drills, favors using instinctive approaches to movement. Improvisation is the key and a confidence in your ability to relax whilst under pressure enables the student to move freely and comfortably. Sambo does not use Katas or forms but encourages students to get to know their own bodies, utilizing both fluidity and strength whilst delivering devastating blows, throws and combat techniques. Ultimately, the student develops a style unique to him or her self.

# Sambo is a merger of other martial arts including Judo, Wrestling and traditional folk styles of grappling

*Competitors at the Melbourne Open Sambo Grappling Competition, Australia*

## OLEG TAKTAROV

Growing up in Gorky, Russia, Oleg took up Judo as a child and later Sambo and went on to win world Sambo championships. By the age of 26 he had won everything he entered. He was a chief instructor of hand-to-hand combat in the elite Soviet anti-terrorist unit and decided the USA was the place for him, where he debuted with his first UFC fight and beat champion David "Tank" Abbott in the finals. Oleg went on to become one of MMA's most popular contestants and later appeared in many Hollywood movies.

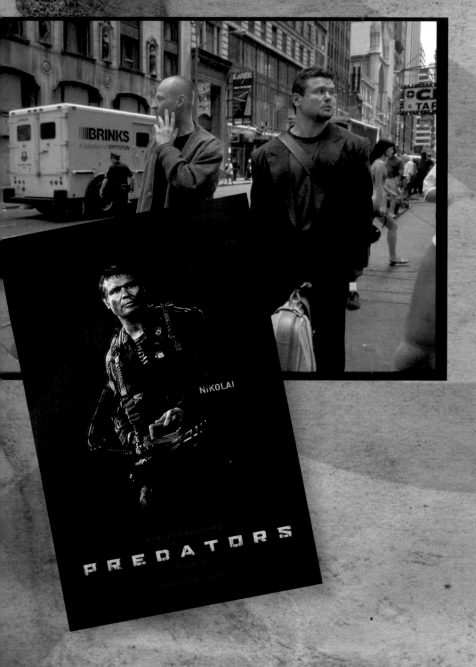

## FEDOR EMELIANENKO

Fedor was born in 1976 in the city of Rubizhne in the Soviet Union. He began his mixed martial arts training by becoming a member of the Russian Top Team. Having trained in Judo and Sambo, he went on to dominate in MMA and Pride fighting for nearly a decade and remained undefeated for that time. He won Gold medals in Combat Sambo, throughout Russia, Europe and in 2002 won The World Combat Sambo Federation title.

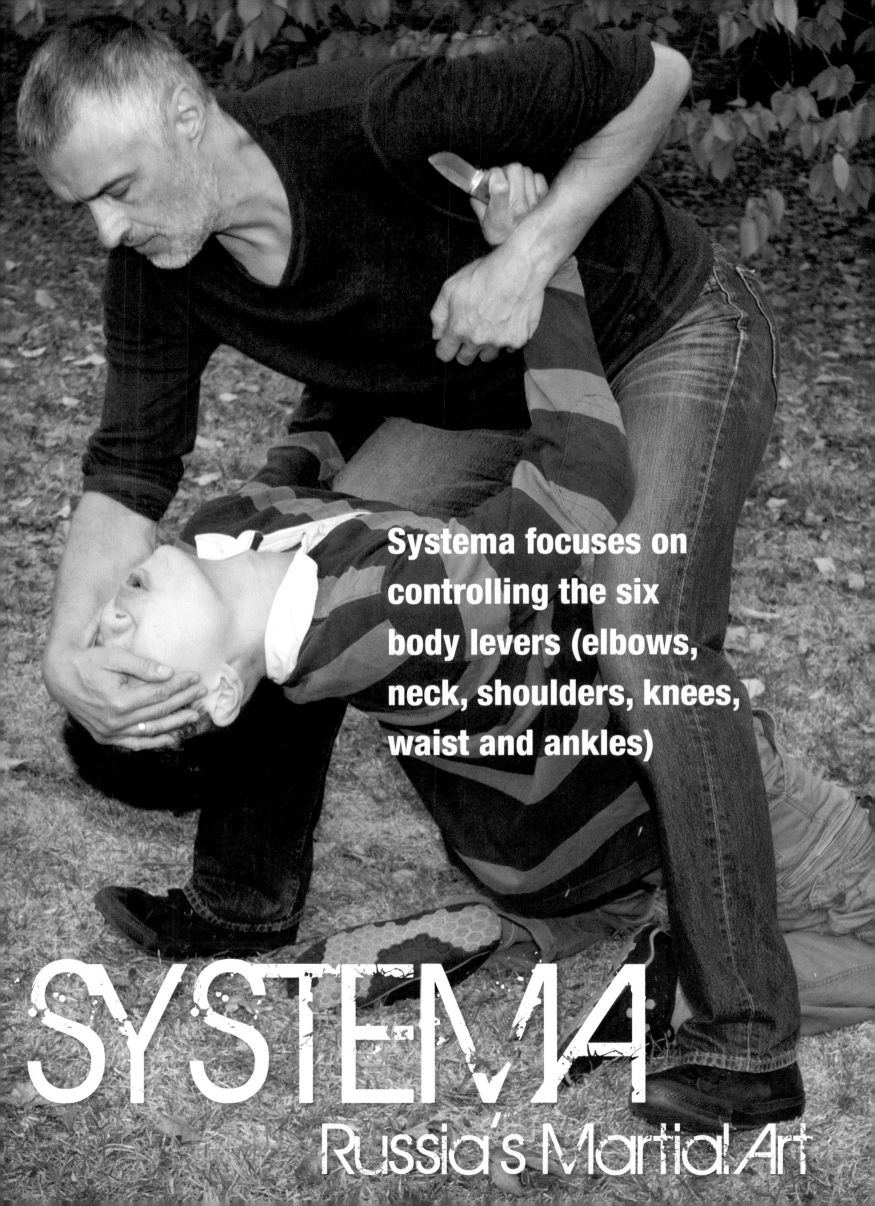

Systema focuses on controlling the six body levers (elbows, neck, shoulders, knees, waist and ankles)

# SYSTEMA
## Russia's Martial Art

Systema, formerly known as Sokoli Stalina, was used by Stalin's personal body guards up until his death in 1953, and then later by the Special Military operations Units for the highest risk missions in the KGB. Close combat training had become the most difficult challenge for all forms of martial arts throughout the world. The goal of Stalin's team called "The Falcons" was to have a system that combined all three levels of human abilities – the physical, the psychological and the psychic. The secret was to develop tactics that would not look like martial actions, and were so subtle that when they were applied it would be difficult to see what happened and how. Exactly opposite to what the martial world was accustomed to seeing in the movies or flashy demonstrations that looked impressive but telegraphed your intention. Systema practitioners are trained to get in very close whilst avoiding triggering alarm bells in the opponent's response system in order to finish the job as quickly and efficiently as possible. No sparring to feel out the opponent is required. The requirements for Systema are very different to sports Sambo or MMA competition, as Systema has been developed for the battlefield.

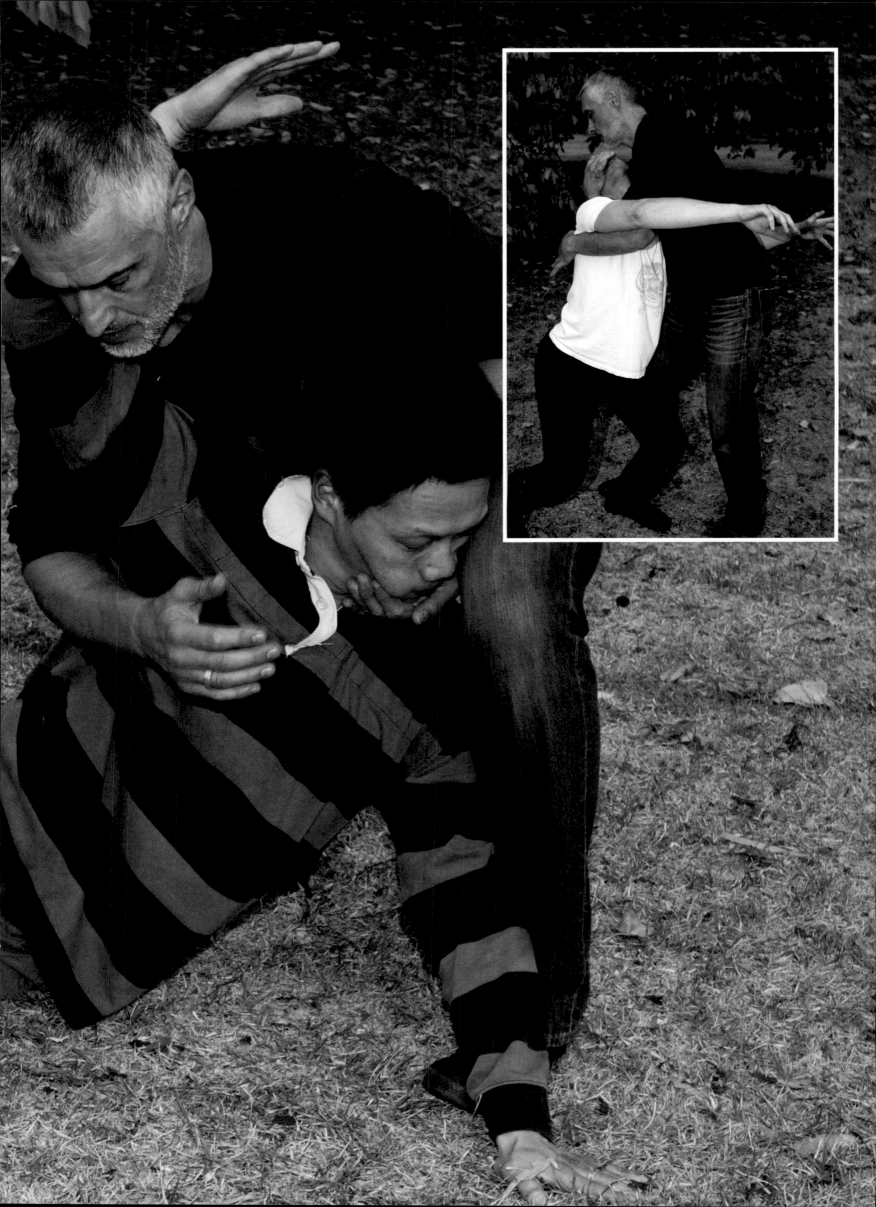

# KUNG FU

## There is no beginning or end to movement

*Master Liu Deming working with iron rings. Each one weighs half a Kilo and training can be up to 3-4 hours at a time to condition the arms.*

少林

It is said that the original form of martial contest in China goes back over 3000 years to a form of wrestling called Horn Butting, where contestants wore helmets with horns on them.

Called Gong Fu in China , it wasn't until Bruce Lee introduced Chinese martial arts to the west that it became known as Kung Fu. Originally from the Shang and Zhou Dynasties (256 BC) the techniques that they used were very basic, comprising of leaping, tumbling and kicking and later introduced weapons made of stone and wood.

Because of the numbers of travelling journeymen, and remembering that firearms were not being used as yet, open handed fighting skills were essential for survival and weaponry was limited to rudimentary instruments. Various styles of boxing, and the development of effective weapons and the mastery of handling them, flourished throughout China. Individuals dedicated their lives to learning great skills of self-defense and movement along with healing, and it was usually the case that a trained martial artist would also practice medicine.

*Shaolin monk practising the ancient art.*

Practitioners were constantly being challenged and would have to apply themselves diligently to keep their edge. Everything was written and catalogued and the Shaolin Temple was known to have an extensive library of everything that the masters had discovered.

What made Kung Fu so unique were the forms created mimicked different fighting styles of birds and animals, e.g. (monkey, bear, snake, tiger or eagle, crane and even insects like the praying mantis). The idea behind this was that in order to survive in the wild these animals used a natural talent and if that could be reproduced it could mean the difference between life and death.

The Chinese martial arts were strongly influenced by Chan Buddism and Taoism in conjuction with traditional Chinese medicine. Gong Fu was a mixture of internal, external, Northern and Southern styles and each one of these had endless styles within them. Internal styles were known as Wu dan and Ermei. External was called Shaolin.

Over hundreds of years, the Chinese governments closed down the Shaolin temple many times and each time it resurfaced, until it was destroyed in 1927 (including all the treasured writings that had been recorded over the years). The monks that could, fled overseas, others went into hiding but most set up schools in both Hong Kong and Taiwan.

Fortunately some of the writings had been kept aside and were published and revealed to the public. Luckily for us many famous masters continued to train and pass on their secrets to their families.

# Kung Fu Techniques

Kung Fu training in China is taken very seriously and most practitioners that excel usually started as children. The old-school methods of training were extremely harsh but the standard was very high. It was not uncommon for wealthy parents to seek out schools like the Chinese Opera, where the students were not only taught theatrical skills but also acrobatics and Wushu fighting.

After many years of practicing fighting techniques, punching and kicking and performing sets of movements, the student is taught to free spar. Before a student can do this successfully they must understand that it is not a free for all with both students burying their heads and swinging at random.

First you must be able to apply all the techniques that you have been practicing whilst under pressure and whilst you are being attacked. You must also be able to arrange certain techniques into short specific sequences whilst maintaining your balance, gradually releasing pre-rehearsed responses so you can improvise. This is done by introducing variations or changes according to the circumstances.

*Master Liu and his students practising freestyle sparring using techniques practised in class*

# Conditioning

The conditioning of the body is essential and young students are taught to stretch and strengthen allowing them to eventually move with little limitation in whatever style they practice. Strong stances, blinding fast responses with punches, kicks, tumbles and somersaults are all used in combat. Combining this with Chi Gung exercises helps students to remain calm , develop sensitivity and remove tension.

Masters practice cleverly combining defense and attack and see it as one, linking it to the philosophy of Yin and Yang and movement having no beginning or end.

# Style

There are endless variations of styles within the Kung Fu system some that evolved naturally from the environment and surroundings . The people from the north of China where it is known for being cold and having large open spaces are usually bigger in size and their actions usually mimick that with larger movements. In the south where the climate is warmer there are more hills and limited space the people are generally more compact and a shorter style of fighting was developed where the artists develops skills to get in very close and deliver shorter blows.

Some popular styles are: Choy lee Fut, Wing Chun, White crane andless known in the west are Shaolin chang Yuun, Lin he ,Ziranmen, Xinji, Ba Gua and Tai Chi .

Much like the Kata in Karate, Kung Fu has forms or sets of movements that are

designed not only to exercise the body but also to train the mind to remember the sequence as they are all fighting attacks and responses that appear deceiving, as they look so fluid. Performed at high speed with brilliant precision, rolling on the ground and jumping through the air the student moves with a mixture of grace and power that is not only impressive to watch but for the practitioner builds fitness, strength and awareness, whilst constantly making use of acting imagination as he or she visualizes being attacked and repeating the form endlessly to refine and perfect it. The next stage is an advanced level where students perform a choreographed series of attacks and responses presented in a form to get them used to space relationship with an opponent before moving on to free sparring.

# JUDO

柔道

## Maximum efficiency, minimum effort

*Judo founder Kano Jigoro*

Like most of the Japanese martial arts, Judo's roots came from Jujitsu. Judo was first established in 1882 with a combination of jujitsu moves and Sumo techniques.

Originally developed from the Samurai warriors, Jujitsu was developed for close quarters hand-to-hand combat on the battlefield if by chance the warrior was caught out without his weapons. As Japan started to integrate with the west, Jujitsu started to decline and if it wasn't for Jigoro Kano - known as the founder of Judo - we would not have this wonderful sport today.

Kano was a small frail teenager and decided to join the Tenyin Shin'yo Jujitsu School in an attempt to become stronger under the watchful eye of Yanosuke Fukuda. Kano started to formulate his own opinions about close quarter fighting and before too long found he was using the opponent's energy against them and started to drop some of the more dangerous Jujitsu techniques gaining more acceptance as a sport. At the ripe old age of 21, he opened the first Judo school in Japan, taking what he thought was all the best ingredients from what he had learnt from master Fukuda and the various Jujitsu styles, and with just 9 students proceeded to build a worldwide organisation calling it Kodokan Judo.

Kano decided that Europe would be the first place to introduce his art to outside of Japan, but not everyone was convinced that a man of this stature could do so. On board the ship to Europe, a foreigner made fun of Kano. Before he knew it he was being thrown to the ground with Kano catching his head with his hand preventing the man from serious injury. Word spread about this incident and helped develop a way to learn a martial art through teamwork and a friendly environment.

In 1886, a competition was held between Jujitsu and Judo. Kano's students won easily, with Kano working tirelessly to promote his sport. Eventually in 1910, Judo became a recognized sport and the following year was included in Japan's education system.

In 1921 the Judo Medical Research Society was born and about this time the Judo syllabus was changed, reducing the amount of throws from 48 to 40..

The emphasis on working on yourself as a contributor to society and the community was encouraged, with moral and spiritual training added to the physical training of Judo.

In 1964 Judo was accepted as an Olympic sport at the Tokyo Olympics.

As the founder, Kano was awarded a doctorate degree that was seen as equivalent to a 12th dan. Those who had the fortune to train with him said it was like fighting an empty jacket. Kano devoted his life to Judo and at the age of 78 died of pneumonia aboard the S.S. *Hikawa* in 1938.

Judo is now practised by millions of men, women and children worldwide and was recently represented by 135 countries at the London Olympics. Students learn how to maintain balance, co-ordination, exercise, self protection and self confidence.

Judo is a combative system where people fight on a padded mat with the idea being to win decisively using a throw or a grappling technique. The two guiding principles are maximum efficient use of energy and mutual prosperity for self and others. Over the years, the more dangerous techniques have been removed for safety reasons so that competitors can feel confident to not hold back.

## METHODS OF TRAINING

There are 3 primary methods of training. They are Kata's (forms), free practice (including sparring) and competition.

The aim of Kata is to teach different combat principles through pre-planned sets of movements and techniques that have been developed over the years from studying different combat situations. Competition is encouraged as a way to test what you have learned and lectures are also used to enhance the students understanding of theory and knowledge of the details.

## JUDO TECHNIQUES

Judo is known for its spectacular throwing techniques but not so known for its many techniques for controlling an opponent whilst on the ground. Likened to free style wrestling, it is said that the art of Sambo was developed from Judo. Breaking the opponent's balance is one of the objectives of a judo competitor making use of timing and leverage. It is common once you have your opponent on the ground to apply painful pins, chokes and arm locks to control the attacker. If the opponent does not surrender he can have joints dislocated or, if in a chokehold, be rendered unconscious. The idea for the person being thrown is to learn the art of Ukemi that allows you to fall properly and avoid injury. It is one of the few Martial Arts where you use full force to execute a technique with the emphasis on breaking the opponents balance, establishing your position and completing your throw.

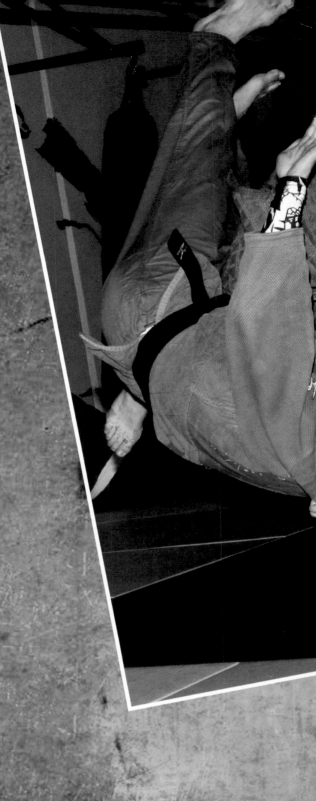

Daniel Kelly 4th Dan Sensei and MMA fighter takes his students through their paces

*Ronda Rousey shows the guys how it is done*

*Ronda Rousey
outside competition*

## Kansetsu Waza - (Arm locks)

The most popular and effective armbar is the cross armlock, called the Crossbar.

And is not only used in competition but also in self-defense. It is particularly effective as you use the whole body including hips and legs against a straightened arm making it possible for a smaller frame person to subdue a larger attacker.

Other powerful armlocks are the Entangled armlock, Trapped elbow armlock, Armpit armlock, Knee armlock and the Knee entangled armlock.

There are 67 throws in Kodokan Judo. From 1920 through to 1982 the Kodokan Gokyo no Waza, which is the standard syllabus of Judo throws, was made up of 40 throws. In 1982, 25 throws were added and later in 1997 the last 2 additional throws completed what is known as the Shinmeiso no Waza.

There have been some wonderful mixed martial artists that had come through the Judo system. Ronda Rousey who learnt how to apply an armbar from anywhere at any time as a kid has become a world champion and is constantly surprising her fans with her talent. Hector Lombard is also leaving his mark on the MMA community competing in Pride; cage fighting, UFC and Bellator. He was also an Olympic judoka. Champions Akiama Yoshihiro and Manny Gamburyan also came from Judo backgrounds.

*Victorian Judo competitors at Pre Nationals Australia*

## ASHI WAZA - Judo Foot Techniques

One of the advantages of the foot sweep is that it can be used whilst a person is advancing or retreating. It works extremely well against a counter and as a set up for your next technique. Popular techniques are the Leg Wheel, Front foot sweep, spring hip counter, Knee wheel hip counter, Lift pull foot sweep, Knee wheel and Minor outer hook.

**Leg Wheel**

**Front Foot Sweep**

**Spring Hip Counter**

**Knee Wheel Hip Sweep Counter**

**Lift Pull Foot Sweep**

**Knee Wheel**

**Minor Outer Hook**

**Minor Outside Reaping Throw**

**Large Wheel**

**Sliding Or Following Foot Sweep**

**Major Outside Reaping Counter**

**Major Outside Reaping Throw**

**Major Outer Wheel**

**Major Outer Drop**

**Major Inner Reaping Counter**

**Major Inner Reaping Throw**

**Lifting Pulling Ankle Throw**

**Swallow Counter**

**Inner Thigh Throw**

**Inner Thigh Throw Counter**

*Victorian Judo competitors at Pre Nationals, Australia*

**The two guiding principles are maximum efficient use of energy and mutual prosperity for self and others**

# WRESTLING
## One of the oldest forms of combat

MMA fighter Zack Hook mixes it up with his freestyle wrestling
coach Champion Konstantin Ermakovich

Most of us are aware of World Championship Wrestling with its awesome publicity machine and its faithful fans. The only time we really hear or see anything apart from that, is every four years when we are watching the Olympics and see some fantastic footage of what is known as Greco Roman wrestling or Freestyle wrestling. Freestyle has become extremely popular in mixed martial arts circles and with UFC competitors, and one of the most common questions asked is what is the difference?

Research tells us that Greco-Roman is practiced only by men whereas in freestyle, men and women participate. Both styles use grappling,, but there are numerous differences with takedowns and what can be used in competitions. The main difference in freestyle wrestling is both parties can use their legs for offensive and defensive work sometimes throwing their opponent to the ground and then reconnecting with them after the throw to apply a hold.

## GRECO-ROMAN

In Greco-Roman wrestling, the use of legs to take someone to the ground is not permitted. In fact you cannot grab below the waist at all making it very challenging to secure a takedown.

The idea behind this sport is for two competitors to attempt to gain control over their opponent through the application of throws, locks and clinching, making it difficult as mentioned because of the no clenching below the waist rule. The goal is to pin the opponent's shoulders to the mat. This is known as victory by fall. Greco-Roman wrestling first appeared at the Olympic Games in Athens in 1896 and is still practiced today.

*Photographed at In2Fitness Martial Arts Centre*

Most people think that this style of wrestling came about from ancient times because of the name, but it has its origins in the 19th century and was originally known as "flat hand wrestling" to separate it from other combative sports that allowed hits. It was also known as French wrestling.

The weight divisions range from 55kg to 120kg. There is a tendency to use powerful throws to take an opponent to the ground. The most popular is the "suplex", where the wrestler lifts the opponent in a high arch falling backwards onto his own neck to bring his opponents shoulders to the mat. Professional matches earned a reputation for their brutality, with a totally different rule structure to what we know today. Body slams, chokes and head butting were allowed but over the years a more sensible approach was applied.

## HOW DO YOU WIN?

1.  A fall. Known as the win by fall or pin is when a Greco-Roman wrestler pins his opponent's shoulders to the mat for long enough for the referee to see the total control of the fall. The mat chairman or judge concurs with the referee that the fall is made.

2.  By injury, withdrawal, default, disqualification of the opponent.

3.  By technical superiority

4.   By points (winning two periods by 1 to 5 points difference)

Competitors in Greco-Roman wrestling are very strong with their ability to clinch, and in the clinch the wrestler has a great number of takedowns, throws and suplexes. The battle for underhooks and the proper use of overhooks are paramount with this style. The upright posture that takes place in Greco-Roman wrestling transfers well to MMA fighting as unlike Judo throws there is no jacket to grip or clench. On the ground Greco-Roman wrestlers shine and are extremely skilled at controlling and pinning their opponents to the mat. There have been many practitioners of this style that have made the shift to MMA successfully including Randy Couture, Dan Henderson and Matt Lindland all excelling in UFC.

Freestyle wrestling is believed to originate from Great Britain. It became popular at fairgrounds throughout the 19th century in the USA, where it was known as "Catch-as-catch-can" wrestling. Freestyle wrestling struggled as a sport in the early years as Greco-Roman was seen as the real deal at the time. In 1904, it made its first appearance at the Olympic Games with all forty competitors coming from the USA. Taking place on a thick rubber mat that is shock absorbent to ensure safety, the main wrestling area is nine meters in diameter and is surrounded by a 1.5-meter border called the protection area. Inside the 9 meter in diameter circle is a red band at 1 meter called the passivity zone. The match takes place between two opponents of the same weight and has three by two minute rounds. A wrestler wins when they have won two out of three periods or if they manage a pin fall during the match.

If at the end of a two-minute round, the scores are 0-0, both competitors go into an overtime period called The Clinch.

# Techniques

Leg attacks are a great way to take down your opponent and of course it depends on your style of wrestling and your body type what techniques are suitable for each individual. Low level leg attacks suit lightweight wrestlers as they are extremely fast at changing levels. The aim is to attack the ankles or feet and there are numerous ways to do this.

A very effective low level attack is known as the Sweep Single, where the attack is focused on the opponent's foot or ankle. The attacker uses an outside penetration step to attack the leg by dropping to one knee and leaving the other leg reasonably straight to push off from, once the hands are placed correctly. The hands wrap around the ankle and you should be facing the same direction as your opponent with your head resting on his hip. You then use your body to drive into his hip whilst securing his ankle.

## THE ANKLE PICK

This technique requires you to be accurate and have good timing. Whilst controlling your opponent's head or upper body, the attacker scoops his hand behind the opponent's heel and projects his bodyweight - including his head - forward, taking him off balance and to the mat. This is sometimes called "The Head and Heel"

## MID-LEVEL ATTACKS

### The Double Leg Take Down

Commonly used by wrestlers of all weights because of the success rate, the idea is to take your opponent off balance by getting in close enough to wrap your hands around your opponent's legs, behind the knees, keeping your elbows in when approaching. Drop one knee to the ground and as you do, make sure your shoulder hits your opponent's hips, sending him back. Your hands snake themselves down to the calves and as you project your shoulder forward, pull their legs toward you.

### High Crotch Take Down

This technique is very similar to the Double leg takedown but the attacking wrestler does not grab on the outside of the legs but reaches inside and takes control of one of the opponent's legs. Your head needs to be in the correct position for this technique to be effective. Attempt to stay forehead to forehead with your opponent. Grip your opponent's elbow, that is on the

same side of the body as the lead leg, with whatever arm is closest, keeping your thumb on the outside of your opponent's arm. Maintain a low, staggered stance with the back leg planted firmly behind you. Bend your knees and lower your body and pull your opponent's elbow over your shoulder, this will reduce the distance between you and enable you to secure your opponents front leg faster.